KELSEY GRAMMER BIOGRAPHY

Behind the Voice, Beyond the Screen:
A Journey Through Fame, Tragedy,
and Triumph

MATTHEW J. PINKLEY

Copyright © 2025 by Matthew J. Pinkley

All rights reserved. No part of this publication may be reproduced, distributed, or transmitted in any form or by any means, including photocopying, recording, or electronic or mechanical methods, without the prior written permission of the author, except in the case of brief quotations embodied in critical reviews and certain other noncommercial uses permitted by copyright law.

TABLE OF CONTENTS

INTRODUCTION: THE MAN BEHIND THE CURTAIN. 4
- The Familiar Voice of an Era...4
- Why His Story Still Matters.. 8
- A Life of Contrasts: Fame and Fragility........................12

CHAPTER 1: ORIGINS OF A VOICE............................... 18
- Caribbean Childhood and American Dreams.................. 18
- A Family Shattered: Losses That Defined Him.............. 22
- Finding Solace in Shakespeare and Stagecraft................ 27

CHAPTER 2: THE RISE OF A COMIC GIANT............. 32
- The Birth of Frasier Crane..32
- Cheers to Stardom: The Power of a Supporting Role..... 37
- Frasier: Carrying a Series, Creating a Legacy.................41

CHAPTER 3: CHAOS BEHIND THE CURTAIN............ 47
- Addiction, Arrests, and the Tabloid Circus...................... 47
- Public Persona vs. Private Pain... 52
- Friends, Foes, and Fragile Reputations............................. 56

CHAPTER 4: REINVENTION IN A RELENTLESS INDUSTRY.. 62
- Producer, Director, Risk-Taker.. 62
- Voice Work and Unexpected Roles................................... 67
- Resurrecting Frasier: Nostalgia and Renewal.................. 71

CHAPTER 5: FAITH, FAMILY, AND FORWARD MOTION..77
- Spiritual Anchors and Personal Redemption....................77
- Love, Loss, and Life After the Storm...............................81

The Enduring Power of Purpose..86
CONCLUSION: THE ECHO OF A SINGULAR LIFE.. 91
Legacy Etched in Laughter and Pain...............................91
A Voice That Transcended Generations.......................... 95
Beyond the Screen: The Triumph of Becoming Whole.. 99

INTRODUCTION: THE MAN BEHIND THE CURTAIN

The Familiar Voice of an Era

Long before streaming platforms fragmented television audiences and algorithms shaped what we watch, the American sitcom reigned supreme. In that golden age of network television, one voice rose above the noise—a voice that was both erudite and dryly comedic, soothing yet sharply articulate. It was the voice of Dr. Frasier Crane, a character who first appeared as a supporting role on Cheers but eventually became the defining sound of a television generation. That voice belonged to Kelsey Grammer, and over time, it became inseparable from the man himself.

Grammer's vocal performance didn't just carry a show; it defined an archetype. He was the urbane intellectual in a world of slapstick humor, the sophisticated cynic navigating a landscape of emotional chaos. His clipped diction, baritone richness, and dramatic cadence gave Frasier an identity far deeper than the scripts alone could convey. It was a masterclass in voice acting though it wasn't animated, it might as well have been for how powerfully his voice shaped the character's soul.

To say his voice became iconic would be an understatement. For over two decades, audiences invited it into their homes weekly. From Cheers (1984–1993) to Frasier (1993–2004), Grammer played Dr. Crane for 20 consecutive years—a television record at the time for a single character portrayed by the same actor. During that run, he didn't just become a star—he became a staple of American popular culture. His voice signaled a certain kind of comedy: intelligent, neurotic, class-conscious, and tinged with just enough tragedy to feel real.

But what made Grammer's voice so captivating wasn't merely its tonal beauty or theatrical training—it was the vulnerability that lay beneath it. There was always a sense, in the way he delivered even the most sarcastic lines, that Frasier Crane (and by extension, Grammer) was searching for something: connection, validation, peace. It's what made his rants endearing rather than grating, his arrogance tolerable rather than repellent. His voice carried the weariness of someone who'd seen too much, even if his character's troubles were often wrapped in farce.

This duality comedy cloaked in melancholy—mirrored Grammer's real life more closely than fans might have imagined. Off-screen, he had weathered unimaginable personal tragedies: the murder of his father, the rape and murder of his sister, the deaths of half-brothers. These events left scars that no fame could fully heal. And while the audience heard a flawless performance week after week, those who listened closely could sometimes detect the echoes of something deeper, something that felt like grief transformed into art.

In an era before prestige dramas explored the intricacies of trauma and identity, Grammar brought complexity to mainstream television. He turned the "funny shrink" into a vehicle for existential exploration. The irony, of course, was that in playing a radio psychiatrist—someone whose job was to soothe others with advice and insight—Grammer, through Frasier, was unwittingly soothing audiences with his own presence. His voice became a kind of cultural therapy: reliable, familiar, safe.

In addition to television, Grammar lent his voice to numerous animated series, most famously as the villainous Sideshow Bob on The Simpsons. Again, his voice work stood out—not for its villainy, but for its Shakespearean grandeur. Sideshow Bob wasn't just a caricature of a criminal; he was an opera-loving, overly articulate, emotionally tortured being. And only Grammar could make that absurdity feel profound.

In many ways, his voice became his brand. It gave him access to work even when his personal life was in turmoil. Studios trusted it. The Audience loved it. Critics praised it. And as technology advanced and TV formats changed, it remained one of the few constants in an ever-shifting media landscape.

Even today, in reruns and reboots, his voice retains its power. It transports people—not just to a specific time in their lives, but to a feeling. A time when television had room for cleverness and depth, when a character could spend an entire episode trying to recite Shakespeare or untangle the psychology of his own ego, and somehow still be funny. A time when the sound of Kelsey

Grammer's voice meant it was okay to laugh, think, and feel all at once.

Ultimately, the voice of an era isn't just one that's heard often. It's one that resonates—through time, through space, and through the hearts of those who heard it. Kelsey Grammer didn't just entertain. He narrated a generation.

Why His Story Still Matters

In the vast landscape of Hollywood biographies, it's easy to overlook stories that seem already told—especially when they belong to familiar faces from long-running sitcoms. But Kelsey Grammer's story defies simplicity. It is not just a tale of fame, but of survival. Not just a story of laughter, but of loss, reinvention, and redemption. His journey holds enduring relevance in an age that both glorifies celebrity and craves authenticity. His story still matters—perhaps now more than ever.

Why? Because his life is a mirror for the contradictions that define the human experience. On screen, Grammar embodied intelligence, wit, and control. Off screen, his world often spiraled into chaos. Substance abuse, multiple failed marriages, arrests, personal tragedies—these headlines followed him like a shadow. And yet, he kept working. He kept showing up. In an industry that is merciless with its fallen stars, Grammar remained if bruised unbowed.

His persistence in the face of pain is not merely a celebrity comeback narrative. It is emblematic of something deeper: the universal struggle to find meaning after devastation. Grammer's story is riddled with almost mythic suffering. His father was murdered when he was thirteen. Just seven years later, his sister was abducted, raped, and killed in an act of horrific violence. Two half-brothers would later die in a freak scuba diving accident. These tragedies didn't just haunt his past; they became the emotional undercurrent of his entire life. Few public figures carry a history that dark—and fewer still manage to maintain a career so steeped in joy and comedy.

In that contradiction lies his importance. Grammer's life is proof that grief does not erase humor. That artistry can spring from agony. That the human spirit, while not invincible, is astonishingly resilient. In an era that increasingly values vulnerability and emotional transparency, his journey reads as a kind of blueprint: not perfect, but profoundly human.

Moreover, Grammer's relevance extends into the cultural conversation about masculinity, trauma, and mental health. For years, he played a character—Dr. Frasier Crane—who was intellectual, emotional, and unabashedly flawed. He helped normalize the idea of men talking about their feelings, going to therapy, and struggling with self-worth. Though cloaked in comedy, Frasier's insecurities were real, and Grammer's portrayal made them approachable. At a time when television often reduced men to caricatures of toughness or cluelessness, Grammar offered a third option: the neurotic, introspective, emotionally complicated man. It was a revolution in its own way.

His influence also matters within the broader context of television history. As the star of one of the most critically acclaimed spin-offs in history, he helped shape what long-form character development could look like on the small screen. Frasier wasn't just a successful show—it was a blueprint for balancing highbrow humor with accessible warmth. It proved that smart television could also be successful television. The series won 37 Emmy Awards and ran for 11 seasons, earning its place in TV history. And at the center of it all was Grammar—crafting a performance that was sharp, complex, and deeply affecting.

But beyond the accolades and the screen, his story matters because it's not finished. Grammer has never stopped evolving. He didn't retreat from the spotlight after Frasier. Instead, he expanded his creative reach, producing shows like Girlfriends and Medium, and taking on dramatic roles that distanced him from the Frasier persona. He returned to Broadway, embraced voice acting, and even entered the world of politics and business. While some actors faded after their peak, Grammer refused to be reduced to his most famous role. His willingness to reinvent himself—not for reinvention's sake, but out of creative necessity—makes him a compelling figure even now.

Perhaps most importantly, his story matters because he never pretended it didn't. Grammer never tried to whitewash his past. He spoke openly about his substance abuse, his grief, and his failings. Not to gain sympathy, but to own them. In a culture that often punishes imperfection, his candor is refreshing—and instructive. He is a reminder that fallibility does not negate worth. That a person can be many things at once: brilliant and broken, loved and loathed, iconic and intensely human.

In the end, Kelsey Grammer's story is not just the story of a man who made us laugh. It's the story of a man who endured. Who kept working when the world gave him every reason to give up. Who used his voice not only to entertain, but to survive. And in doing so, he gave voice however unconsciously to the struggles so many carry in silence.

That's why his story still matters. Because it isn't just about a celebrity. It's about all of us.

A Life of Contrasts: Fame and Fragility

Kelsey Grammer's life is a portrait painted in stark contrasts. At a glance, he appears as the quintessential success story—a man who brought one of television's most beloved characters to life, who stood atop Hollywood's summit for decades, and who won multiple Emmy and Golden Globe awards while making it all look effortless. Yet beneath that glittering surface lies a more complex truth: Grammer's journey has been shadowed by personal loss, emotional turmoil, and a relentless battle for stability. He is a man who has lived at the peak of celebrity and the pit of despair, often at the same time. Fame and fragility have walked side by side through nearly every chapter of his life.

To the public, he was the unshakably witty Dr. Frasier Crane, a man of refined tastes, sharp intelligence, and comic timing so precise it became iconic. His on-screen presence exuded confidence and class. Viewers came to rely on his familiar face and voice as a source of comfort and humor. Few could imagine that behind the scenes, Grammer was often clinging to emotional and psychological survival. The same man who delivered polished monologues about love and loneliness on Frasier was, in reality, enduring breakdowns, substance abuse, and suicidal despair.

These opposing realities public success and private suffering define Grammer's story. His life is not a straightforward climb to the top, nor is it a tragic downfall. It is a tangled, ongoing journey that veers between triumph and trauma. And it is in this very duality that his story gains depth and resonance.

Grammer's early life set the stage for this contrast. Raised in St. Thomas in the U.S. Virgin Islands, he seemed destined for a life shaped by art. He found joy in performance at a young age and trained at the prestigious Juilliard School. But even then, fragility crept in through unimaginable loss. At 13, he lost his father to a brutal murder. A few years later, his sister was abducted, raped, and murdered in one of the most horrifying crimes in Colorado's history. These events, compounded by the accidental deaths of his half-brothers years later, created an emotional landscape few could navigate. The fragility born of that trauma never left him; it simply coexisted with the talent that drove him forward.

By the time he became a household name on Cheers, Grammer was already struggling with substance abuse—alcohol and cocaine became his means of coping with grief and pressure. Even as he was being lauded for his comedic brilliance, he was spiraling behind closed doors. The media covered his legal troubles, his car accidents, and stints in rehab with the typical blend of voyeurism and judgment reserved for troubled celebrities. What the headlines missed, however, was the human being at the center of it all—a man cracking under the weight of sorrow and expectation.

And yet, this fragility didn't define him. It shaped him, but it didn't stop him. One of the most compelling aspects of Grammer's life is his refusal to surrender to despair. He never abandoned his craft, never stepped away from the stage or the screen for long. He leaned into his work not just as a profession but as a lifeline. Acting became both a mask and a mirror—allowing him to hide from his pain while also expressing it through the characters he played. Frasier Crane, in many ways, became an extension of himself: neurotic, eloquent, perpetually seeking love and connection, often lost in his own mind.

Outside of acting, his life continued to swing between extremes. His personal relationships were often volatile—marked by multiple marriages, custody battles, and heartbreak. And yet he remained an active father, eventually finding a quieter sense of family life in later years. Spiritually, he moved toward faith, speaking openly about his Christian beliefs and the role they played in his healing. Professionally, he expanded into producing, voice acting, and theater—continuing to evolve even as the industry changed around him.

Grammer's life reveals a truth we often resist: that fragility and strength are not opposites. They are partners. His fame did not protect him from suffering, and his fragility did not prevent him from achieving greatness. He exists in the overlap, in the space where human beings most often live—not in extremes, but in contradiction.

And that is why his story continues to resonate. It isn't just about a man who made us laugh. It's about a man who refused to let his pain define his worth, who wrestled with his demons under the spotlight, and who emerged, not unscathed, but unbroken. Kelsey Grammer's life is proof that even in the most glamorous narratives, there is room for vulnerability and that fragility does not diminish fame, but rather, deepens its meaning.

CHAPTER 1: ORIGINS OF A VOICE

Caribbean Childhood and American Dreams

Long before the bright lights of Hollywood or the soundstages of network sitcoms, Kelsey Grammer's story began on the windswept shores of the Caribbean—a world away from the spotlight he would one day command. Born Allen Kelsey Grammer on February 21, 1955, in Saint Thomas of the U.S. Virgin Islands, his early years were steeped in the rhythms of island life, surrounded by turquoise seas and sun-drenched skies. But this seemingly idyllic setting was also marked by instability, foreshadowing the turbulence that would come to define much of his personal journey.

The son of Frank Allen Grammer Jr., a musician and owner of a coffee shop and bar and grill, and Sally Cranmer, a singer and actress, Kelsey came into a world already attuned to performance and artistic expression. Creativity ran in his blood. His mother, in particular, recognized early on her son's sensitive disposition and expressive nature. These traits would become central to his identity as both a person and performer. Yet even from childhood, life did not allow Grammer the luxury of security.

When Kelsey was only two years old, his parents divorced. The young boy remained in the care of his mother, and the two shared a close bond that would carry them through years of dramatic upheaval. After the divorce, Sally moved with her son to New Jersey, but before long they relocated once again—this time back to Saint Thomas. These frequent moves underscored a deeper theme in Grammer's early life: transience. His world was always shifting, and with each move came a new attempt to find something resembling home.

Saint Thomas was both a refuge and a proving ground. Life on the island offered Grammer natural beauty and space for imagination, but it also came with isolation. He often spent long stretches of time alone, turning to books, music, and his own imagination to fill the silence. In many ways, these lonely stretches cultivated the inner world that would later fuel his artistry. He began reading Shakespeare as a child, fascinated not just by the stories but by the language—the rhythm, the gravitas, the emotional scope. Even at a young age, he felt drawn to roles that demanded emotional depth and complexity. It was an early signal of the actor he would become.

However, this period of relative calm was tragically disrupted in 1968 when Kelsey was just thirteen. His father, who had remained in Saint Thomas, was shot and killed in a random act of violence just outside his home. The murder was a shock not just to Grammar, but to the fragile foundation of his world. His father's death marked the first major trauma in a life that would be marred by multiple tragic losses. For Kelsey, it planted the first seeds of emotional darkness that would linger in the years to come.

Despite this, Grammar pressed forward. With his mother's encouragement, he pursued an education that emphasized both discipline and creativity. He enrolled at Pine Crest School in Fort Lauderdale, Florida—an elite private prep school where he found both challenge and opportunity. There, he began to seriously consider acting as more than a pastime. Encouraged by his teachers and moved by the works of classic playwrights, he auditioned for and earned roles in school productions. For the first time, he saw acting not just as something he loved but as something he could do—and do exceptionally well.

The stage became a place where he could channel the grief and confusion that followed him from the Caribbean. Each role was a catharsis. Each performance, a release. While many of his peers prepared for conventional careers, Kelsey dreamt of stages, scripts, and the chance to inhabit lives beyond his own. Acting, he realized, was not just an escape—it was a bridge between pain and purpose.

That dream eventually led him to New York City and, later, to the prestigious Juilliard School, where he would hone his craft among the most promising performers of his generation. But before the Broadway lights or television studios, before the red carpets and Emmy Awards, there was an island boy reading Shakespeare under the Caribbean sun—yearning for more than the life he had been handed, dreaming of a world where his voice would be heard.

Kelsey Grammer's Caribbean childhood was not just a backdrop to his success, it was its origin. It instilled in him a sense of beauty and solitude, of rhythm and reflection. And perhaps most importantly, it taught him that art could grow even in the shadow of tragedy. From the shores of Saint Thomas to the stages of America, his journey began with the simple yet powerful belief that a different life one shaped by passion and expression was possible.

A Family Shattered: Losses That Defined Him

For many actors, emotional depth is a skill—something studied, rehearsed, and fine-tuned. For Kelsey Grammer, it was a lived experience. Long before he delivered Frasier Crane's soulful soliloquies or embodied the complex characters of stage and screen, Grammar knew the terrain of grief in a way few people, let alone public figures, could fathom. His life was not simply touched by tragedy, it was reshaped by it, again and again, in brutal and irreversible ways. His family wasn't just broken; it was shattered. And from that wreckage, he built a career steeped in emotional truth.

The first and perhaps most jarring rupture came when Kelsey was just 13. In 1968, his father, Frank Allen Grammer Jr., was murdered in a senseless act of violence outside his home in Saint Thomas. A man named Arthur B. Niles—later deemed criminally insane—set fire to Frank's car to lure him outside, then shot him twice. The murder left Kelsey reeling. He had already experienced emotional turbulence from his parents' divorce and the instability of frequent moves, but this was different. This was permanent. Irreversible. At an age when most boys are still figuring out who they are, Kelsey was forced to confront mortality, evil, and loss.

The trauma might have been enough to derail anyone's emotional development. But for Grammar, it was only the beginning of a much darker sequence. Seven years later, in 1975, his younger sister Karen—only 18 years old—was abducted, raped, and murdered in Colorado Springs. The crime was so horrific it haunted headlines for weeks. Karen, a sweet and hopeful young woman who shared Kelsey's artistic spirit, had gone to wait for a friend after work. She was lured by Freddie Glenn and two accomplices—men who were already on a violent spree. They took her to an abandoned building, where she was sexually assaulted and then stabbed multiple times. Before she died, she reportedly begged them to let her pray.

The grief nearly broke Grammer. Karen was not just his sister—she was one of the last emotional anchors in his life. He had helped raise her after their father's death and their mother's long work hours. Losing her in such a brutal fashion compounded the trauma he was still processing from seven years before. In interviews years later, Grammer would describe how the pain of losing Karen never truly faded. He would say it often felt like he had failed her that his role as her protector had been torn from him.

The pain didn't stop there. In the early 1980s, two of Grammer's half-brothers died in a freak scuba diving accident off the coast of the Virgin Islands. Stephen and Billy, sons from his father's second marriage, had been exploring a coral reef when equipment failure and inexperience led to a tragic end. One drowned outright;

the other disappeared and was never found. Yet again, Grammer was left to mourn—not just the individuals, but the very idea of family itself.

These cumulative losses left scars deeper than most people could understand. And like many who carry unresolved trauma, Grammar turned to escape. Drugs and alcohol became both shield and sword—numbing the pain while slowly chipping away at his well-being. His struggle with addiction would go on to define much of his adult life, leading to multiple rehab stints, DUIs, and public collapses. Yet beneath those destructive choices was a man still trying to make sense of a past filled with ghosts.

It's easy to look at Grammer's life and see contradictions: a man who made millions laugh while suffering silently. But what becomes clear, especially when viewed through the lens of his losses, is that his performances were not divorced from his pain—they were shaped by it. Every note of longing in Frasier's voice, every moment of vulnerability on screen, came from a place of deep, lived experience. He didn't have to imagine grief. He carried it with him into every role.

Even decades later, the impact of those family tragedies lingered. Grammer has spoken openly about how he still dreams about his sister. How he sometimes sees her in his children. How he's had to learn to live with the pain rather than move past it. In 2009, when his sister's killer was up for parole, Grammar submitted a powerful victim impact statement. "I miss her in my bones," he wrote. His grief had never dulled, only deepened.

In a world that often sanitizes celebrity stories, reducing them to red carpets and rehab headlines—Grammer's history forces us to reconsider the full human experience behind fame. He is a man who not only lost his family but had to grieve in the public eye. A man who turned suffering into strength, and somehow found a way to build a life, a career, and a legacy out of devastation.

That legacy, forged in tragedy, is one of the reasons his story matters—not because it's sad, but because it's true.

Finding Solace in Shakespeare and Stagecraft

In a life scarred by trauma and personal tragedy, Kelsey Grammer found his first true refuge not in therapy, religion, or fame, but in the words of William Shakespeare. The Bard's centuries-old scripts became both a mirror for his pain and a map out of it—offering clarity, structure, and catharsis to a young man who otherwise struggled to make sense of a chaotic world. Long before he became a household name as Dr. Frasier Crane, Grammer was a student of the stage—an artist who found meaning, identity, and spiritual grounding in the power of performance.

For Grammar, acting was never just about fame. It was about survival. In the wake of his sister Karen's brutal murder and his father's violent death, he began to turn more deeply to literature. Shakespeare's tragedies, in particular, gave shape to his own unspoken grief. In Hamlet, he found a kindred spirit—a man haunted by the death of a parent, struggling to make sense of betrayal and fate. In King Lear, he saw the devastating impact of familial collapse. And in Macbeth, he wrestled with the idea of destiny corrupted by trauma. These weren't just roles to memorize. They were emotional lifelines.

By high school, Grammer was already demonstrating remarkable talent for classical drama. His teachers at Pine Crest School in Fort Lauderdale recognized his intensity and maturity, encouraging him to take the stage. The spotlight suited him not because it fed an ego, but because it provided structure. The lines were already written, the cues predetermined. In a life where nothing felt predictable, the theater offered something sacred: order.

It wasn't long before his passion led him to pursue acting at the highest level. He was accepted into the prestigious Juilliard School in New York City, an institution known for shaping many of the greatest actors of the modern era. At Juilliard, Grammer trained in voice, movement, and text with some of the most rigorous instructors in the field. But more than technical skill, Juilliard demanded introspection. To succeed there meant learning to bring one's full self to a role—emotionally, physically, and intellectually. For Grammer, it was a place where pain could finally be transformed into art.

Unfortunately, his time at Juilliard would be cut short. After the death of his sister, Grammar struggled to stay focused and disciplined. The emotional weight he carried made it difficult to fully immerse himself in the intensive curriculum. He left Juilliard without graduating, but the experience nonetheless left a deep and lasting mark on his craft. The training gave him a foundation that would set him apart from his peers—particularly in television, where few sitcom actors of the era had classical theater backgrounds.

His early years as a working actor saw him return to Shakespeare again and again, performing in productions of Othello, Macbeth, and Henry V. His deep baritone, sharp diction, and emotional intensity made him a natural for the stage. Audiences and directors took note. Though he was not yet famous, Grammer was respected among theater professionals for his seriousness and commitment to the work. He wasn't trying to be a star; he was trying to be great.

Stagecraft, especially Shakespeare, did more than hone his skills—it gave him a framework for understanding his life. In Shakespeare's characters, Grammar discovered that emotional contradiction was not only normal—it was necessary. Love and rage could exist in the same breath. Grief and strength could live in the same soul. Through performance, he could channel his own trauma into something resonant and redemptive. It allowed him to express what he could not say aloud: his sorrow, his guilt, his longing for justice and peace.

Even after his transition to television and film, the lessons of the stage never left him. His portrayal of Frasier Crane, though comedic, bore traces of Shakespearean roots. The verbosity, the introspection, the dramatic overreactions—they were all crafted with the same discipline he learned at Juilliard and on the boards of classical theater. More importantly, they were infused with real emotion, filtered through a life that had known unimaginable loss. Viewers may not have realized it, but when Grammer performed, he was often telling the truth not necessarily about the plot, but about the depth of human feeling.

In the end, Shakespeare and stagecraft didn't just shape Kelsey Grammer's career, they shaped his identity. They offered him a vocabulary for pain, a stage for transformation, and a sanctuary for the wounded parts of himself. Onstage, he was not a victim of tragedy, but an architect of meaning. Through the ancient words of others, he found his own.

CHAPTER 2: THE RISE OF A COMIC GIANT

The Birth of Frasier Crane

In the vast constellation of American television, few characters have enjoyed the longevity, complexity, and cultural resonance of Dr. Frasier Crane. Introduced in 1984 as a temporary guest star on Cheers, Frasier was initially meant to be little more than a romantic complication—a charming, uptight psychiatrist brought in to ruffle feathers and stir the pot. Yet what began as a short-term role evolved into one of television's most enduring characters, all thanks to the man who gave him voice, depth, and dimension: Kelsey Grammer.

At the time of his casting on Cheers, Grammer was a relatively unknown stage actor. He had spent the early 1980s working in regional theater, honing his Shakespearean chops and developing his distinctive voice—both literally and artistically. While many television actors of the day emerged from sitcom training grounds or improvisational comedy, Grammer came with gravitas. He was steeped in classical training, and that training brought something new to Cheers' familiar formula. When producers Glen and Les Charles, alongside James Burrows, were searching for someone to play Diane Chambers' new love interest, they saw potential in the fresh-faced actor with the commanding baritone.

Frasier Crane first appeared in the Season 3 premiere of Cheers. From the outset, the character was deliberately designed as a foil to Ted Danson's Sam Malone. Where Sam was impulsive and earthy, Frasier was cerebral and restrained. This juxtaposition provided rich comedic potential. But what surprised everyone—from the producers to the audience—was how effortlessly Grammer inhabited the role. He infused Frasier with a mix of pomp and pathos, creating a character that was as exasperating as he was endearing.

The Audience responded. Frasier's elitist vocabulary and overanalyzed anxieties offered something unique amid the working-class bar banter of Cheers. Instead of being written off after a few episodes, Frasier stuck around. Grammer was soon promoted to series regular, and by the time Cheers ended in 1993, Frasier had become a cornerstone of the ensemble.

But Grammer and the producers weren't finished. Rather than retire the character with the end of the beloved Boston-based sitcom, NBC executives—recognizing the growing power of spin-offs—approached Grammer and the Cheers creative team about continuing Frasier's story in a new setting. At first, the idea was met with hesitation. Spin-offs were notoriously difficult to pull off successfully, and there were doubts about whether Frasier's intellectual snobbery could carry an entire show.

The solution lay in reinvention. Rather than keep Frasier in Boston, the new show relocated him to Seattle, Washington. Rather than continue his romantic entanglement with Diane or tie him closely to Cheers' past, the writers gave him a fresh start: a new career as a radio psychiatrist, a strained relationship with his working-class father, and a cast of idiosyncratic new characters—including his brother Niles, played brilliantly by David Hyde Pierce.

Frasier, which debuted in September 1993, was a revelation. It defied all expectations, both creatively and commercially. Within its first season, the show earned critical acclaim and high ratings. It wasn't just funny—it was smart. The scripts were peppered with literary references, classical music, and psychological insights, setting it apart from typical sitcom fare. And at the heart of it all was Grammer's performance. His portrayal of Frasier deepened in this new iteration, evolving from comic side character to richly textured protagonist.

What made Frasier so compelling—especially in Grammer's hands—was his emotional contradiction. He was an intellectual elitist who craved connection, a man trained to understand the human psyche yet constantly baffled by his own relationships. Grammer gave the character soul, often drawing from his personal reservoir of tragedy and resilience. Beneath the laughter was an undercurrent of melancholy—an aching need to be loved and understood. Grammer's Frasier was never a caricature; he was a man trying, and often failing, to live up to his own ideals.

The role brought Grammer unprecedented fame. Over the course of Frasier's 11-season run, he won four Primetime Emmy Awards for Outstanding Lead Actor in a Comedy Series. By the time the series concluded in 2004, he had played Frasier Crane for 20 consecutive years—a record unmatched in television history at the time. The character had not only outlived the show that birthed him but had become one of the most beloved figures in pop culture.

Yet beyond the accolades, Frasier represented something deeper for Grammer: a chance to channel his personal struggles into something lasting. Frasier Crane, with all his flaws, neuroses, and heart, became a vessel for Grammer's own journey. Through the character, he turned pain into performance, grief into grace, and introspection into art.

And so, what began as a side character in a Boston bar became a television titan—born not just from clever writing or lucky casting, but from the singular voice and vision of Kelsey Grammer.

Cheers to Stardom: The Power of a Supporting Role

In the world of television, supporting characters are often written to serve the lead. They arrive with punchlines, offer contrast, and vanish when the central arc demands the spotlight. But occasionally, a supporting character transcends the boundaries of that role, drawing unexpected warmth, curiosity, and resonance from the audience. That was the case with Dr. Frasier Crane on Cheers, and it was Kelsey Grammer's nuanced portrayal that transformed what was meant to be a brief stint into the launching pad of a decades-long television legacy.

When Cheers debuted in 1982, it was a show that didn't immediately find its audience. Centered around the regulars at a Boston bar run by ex-ballplayer Sam Malone (Ted Danson), it initially struggled in the ratings. But as the show found its rhythm—with its ensemble cast, witty scripts, and slow-burning romantic tension between Sam and Diane Chambers (Shelley Long)—it became one of the most beloved sitcoms of the era.

By the time Grammer joined the cast in Season 3, Cheers was already a hit. The showrunners introduced Frasier Crane as a new romantic interest for Diane—a brilliant but socially awkward psychiatrist who would challenge her emotionally and intellectually in ways Sam never could. The plan was simple: Frasier would appear in a few episodes, stir the pot in the Sam-Diane relationship, and then fade away. He wasn't meant to stay.

But Kelsey Grammer had other ideas—none of them conscious, all of them instinctual. From his first lines, Grammar infused Frasier with a mixture of arrogance and vulnerability that made him far more than a simple antagonist or love interest. With his crisp diction, verbose vocabulary, and awkward charm, Frasier wasn't just a wedge in a love triangle—he was a character who felt both unique and strangely familiar. He was pompous but not cruel, brilliant but blind to his own faults, and above all, deeply human.

The audience responded immediately. Rather than reject this new interloper, they embraced him. What might have been an elitist stereotype in lesser hands became a figure of sympathy and humor. It was clear that while

Frasier saw himself as above the fray, he desperately wanted to belong—to be respected, loved, and accepted by his fellow barflies. Grammer played this tension with subtlety, never overreaching for a laugh but allowing Frasier's contradictions to shine through.

Behind the scenes, the writers quickly recognized they had more than a throwaway character on their hands. Frasier offered new comic possibilities, his highbrow sensibilities clashing hilariously with the working-class world of Cheers. His inability to navigate the bar's social dynamics only made him more endearing. And Grammer's performance was effortlessly magnetic—grounded in classical training, yet attuned to sitcom timing.

As the seasons progressed, Frasier evolved from an outsider to an integral part of the ensemble. He developed genuine friendships with characters like Norm, Cliff, and Carla, and his post-breakup interactions with Diane became richer and more layered. Grammer's chemistry with the rest of the cast deepened, and his comedic confidence grew. He no longer felt like a newcomer—he was now one of the reasons people tuned in each week.

This rise from temporary supporting role to beloved series regular is a testament to both character and performer. Grammer didn't steal scenes—he enriched them. He brought depth to dialogue, physicality to intellectualism, and unexpected warmth to a role that could have remained one-dimensional. In doing so, he changed the trajectory of his career.

By the time Cheers ended in 1993, Grammer had spent nearly a decade as Frasier Crane, becoming one of the most recognizable faces on television. He had taken a secondary role and, through consistency, intelligence, and emotional truth, made it unforgettable. It's no exaggeration to say that without Cheers, there would have been no Frasier. And without Grammer, there would have been no Frasier Crane.

What makes this transformation so remarkable is how rare it is. In television history, few supporting characters have leapt so successfully into their own spotlight. But Grammer's Frasier didn't just transition into a lead role—he carried his own show for 11 seasons, winning awards and redefining the sitcom protagonist as a flawed, intellectual soul.

More than just a springboard, Cheers was Grammer's proving ground. It's where he learned to work with an ensemble, navigate the machinery of weekly television, and balance humor with heart. It's where he discovered the extraordinary potential of Frasier Crane. And it's where viewers first fell in love with the voice, the wit, and the vulnerability that would come to define his career.

In that Boston bar, over laughs, love triangles, and long pours, a star was born—not in the center of the frame, but slightly to the side, where the supporting characters live until the audience demands they step forward.

Frasier: Carrying a Series, Creating a Legacy

When Frasier premiered on NBC in 1993, the odds were stacked against it. Spinoffs were a risky proposition—often pale imitations of the originals that failed to stand on their own. Yet Frasier didn't just succeed; it soared, becoming one of the most acclaimed and successful television comedies of all time. At the center of its success was Kelsey Grammer, stepping into the formidable task of transforming a well-loved supporting character into a series lead. What he accomplished was nothing short of extraordinary: not only did he carry the show for 11 seasons, but he also crafted a legacy that continues to influence television to this day.

Grammer's Dr. Frasier Crane had already earned his place in the cultural zeitgeist during his tenure on Cheers. But Frasier marked a rebirth of the character. Relocating him from Boston to Seattle and placing him in a new context—working as a radio psychiatrist while navigating complicated family dynamics—allowed the writers to deepen and reimagine who Frasier really was. No longer the love interest or sidekick, Frasier was now the anchor of a world filled with rich, dynamic characters who each challenged him in unique ways.

The brilliance of Frasier lay in its clever reinvention. It wasn't a bar comedy or a workplace ensemble in the traditional sense. It was, at its heart, a character-driven show about relationships, identity, class, and self-awareness. Frasier's relationship with his blue-collar father Martin (John Mahoney) created the show's emotional spine. Their constant tug-of-war—intellect versus pragmatism, refinement versus simplicity—provided a wellspring of comedic and heartfelt moments. At the same time, the arrival of Frasier's equally neurotic brother Niles (David Hyde Pierce) added layers of rivalry, mirroring, and absurdity that elevated the show's sophistication and charm.

At the center of it all, Grammer's portrayal never faltered. His performance was a masterclass in character continuity and evolution. Despite playing the same role across two separate series, Grammer ensured that Frasier grew and matured. He balanced the character's self-important tendencies with emotional vulnerability and delivered scenes of both slapstick comedy and poignant reflection with equal skill. His background in classical theater allowed him to bring a depth and command that few sitcom actors possessed, and it showed in every monologue, meltdown, and misadventure.

Grammer didn't just perform—he helped shape the tone of the show. His voice, both literally and figuratively, defined Frasier. From the iconic piano theme song ("Tossed Salads and Scrambled Eggs") to the smooth cadence of his radio advice, his delivery became a signature feature. Frasier Crane's vocabulary and mannerisms became comedic trademarks, beloved by fans and endlessly quotable. Yet Grammer never let Frasier become a caricature. Even at his most pompous, the character remained oddly relatable, always yearning for connection and meaning in a world that rarely lived up to his expectations.

Beyond the performance, Grammer's off-camera role in shaping the show grew over time. He eventually became an executive producer, giving him more creative control and deepening his investment in the series' direction. His leadership helped maintain a consistent tone, even as the television landscape evolved and audience tastes shifted. Under his stewardship, Frasier stayed true to its core identity while still allowing for fresh stories and character growth.

The accolades followed. Frasier won five consecutive Emmy Awards for Outstanding Comedy Series, a record at the time, and Grammer himself won four Emmys for Outstanding Lead Actor in a Comedy Series. But the true measure of Frasier's impact lies beyond awards. It offered a rare blend of intellectual humor and emotional intelligence, treating its audience with respect and refusing to dumb down its content. It elevated the sitcom genre, proving that comedy could be sophisticated without losing mass appeal.

By the time Frasier concluded in 2004 after 264 episodes, Grammer had played the character for 20 years—an unprecedented run that set a record in television history. More importantly, he had taken Frasier from a minor role on Cheers to a fully realized, dearly beloved character with a legacy of his own. The show continues to find new audiences through streaming, and in 2023, a revival brought the character back yet again, a testament to his enduring appeal.

Frasier wasn't just a hit sitcom—it was a cultural landmark. And at the heart of it was Kelsey Grammer, who didn't just carry the show but elevated it into something timeless. Through Frasier Crane, he gave the world a character who was laughably flawed, endlessly articulate, and, above all, unmistakably human. That legacy, shaped by Grammer's unwavering commitment and depth, ensures that Frasier will remain a high watermark in the history of television comedy.

CHAPTER 3: CHAOS BEHIND THE CURTAIN

Addiction, Arrests, and the Tabloid Circus

For much of the 1990s and early 2000s, Kelsey Grammer's face was everywhere—on billboards, in television promos, and plastered across the glossy pages of tabloid magazines. As Dr. Frasier Crane, he commanded laughter, accolades, and a towering presence on prime-time television. But behind the carefully polished veneer of comedic brilliance was a man waging a deeply personal war, one that would erupt in public arrests, near-fatal relapses, and a relentless tabloid frenzy that often overshadowed his professional achievements.

Grammer's battles with addiction were not sudden, nor were they the result of fleeting celebrity excess. They were rooted in a complex past of personal loss, trauma, and grief. By the time he was a teenager, he had endured the murder of his father, the brutal killing of his sister, and the tragic deaths of two half-brothers in a scuba accident. These unprocessed traumas left Grammer with a well of pain that would haunt him well into adulthood.

In Hollywood, where masks are easily worn and vulnerability is often seen as weakness, Grammer sought relief in substances. His poison of choice was cocaine, and by his own admission, it offered a temporary escape—a way to numb the anguish that shadowed him. But like so many others caught in addiction, the reprieve was fleeting, and the consequences came fast.

The first public signs of Grammer's descent surfaced in the mid-1980s, not long after he gained popularity on Cheers. In 1988, he was arrested in Malibu for driving under the influence and cocaine possession, earning a 30-day jail sentence. The mugshot—disheveled, hollow-eyed—stood in stark contrast to the suave, composed Frasier Crane that millions adored on television. The media pounced, and Grammer's name began appearing less in entertainment columns and more in police blotters.

But the trouble didn't stop there. In 1990, Grammer was arrested again, this time for cocaine possession and driving under the influence. He was ordered into rehab, and though he completed treatment, the cycle of relapse continued. For a man with immense talent and a flourishing career, these arrests painted a picture of instability and danger. Tabloid headlines turned lurid, dissecting every detail of his missteps. The public watched with equal parts fascination and disappointment, as if witnessing a real-time morality play unfold.

In 1995, Grammer's addiction nearly claimed his life. After a five-day binge, he was found unconscious and rushed to the hospital. Friends feared he would not survive. It was a moment of reckoning—physically, emotionally, and spiritually. The near-death experience was not just another headline; it was a wake-up call, even for a man who had weathered storms his entire life. He entered the Betty Ford Center for rehabilitation, this time with a deeper resolve. It wasn't just about salvaging his reputation—it was about saving his life.

During this time, the dichotomy between Kelsey Grammer the man and Frasier Crane the character became painfully evident. While Frasier dispensed wisdom and poise over the radio airwaves of fictional Seattle, Grammer himself was struggling to stay afloat.

Yet somehow, his performances never faltered. His Emmy-winning work on Frasier continued, even as the headlines raged. Critics marveled at how he could deliver such measured, brilliant performances while fighting inner demons. But perhaps that was part of Grammer's paradox: he was always acting, always surviving, always compartmentalizing the pain.

The media circus reached a fever pitch not just because of the addiction, but also due to Grammer's tumultuous personal relationships. His divorces were messy, his romantic entanglements volatile, and each episode fed the public's insatiable appetite for celebrity scandal. He became a fixture in tabloids like The National Enquirer and People, often reduced to caricature—a gifted actor with a self-destructive streak.

Despite the public shaming and endless speculation, Grammer never entirely disappeared. His talent remained undeniable, and over time, a more nuanced portrait emerged. He began speaking openly about his struggles, acknowledging the pain he had tried to bury and the mistakes he had made along the way. He didn't excuse his behavior, but he did contextualize it—inviting compassion in a culture that often delights in the downfall of the famous.

The path to sobriety wasn't linear. It was filled with relapses, recommitments, and the difficult work of self-confrontation. But over the years, Grammer would begin to rebuild—not just his career, but his identity. The arrests and scandals, while damaging, did not define him. Rather, they became chapters in a larger story: one of endurance, survival, and a deep desire to heal.

In the harsh spotlight of celebrity, many falter and fade. But Kelsey Grammer, for all his failings, never surrendered to the darkness. He faced it—sometimes clumsily, sometimes courageously—and lived to tell the tale. His story is not one of simple redemption, but of complex, ongoing reckoning. It is this honesty that makes his journey resonate far beyond the tabloids—and perhaps, beyond even Frasier Crane.

Public Persona vs. Private Pain

Kelsey Grammer spent much of his career inhabiting the role of Dr. Frasier Crane—urbane, witty, intellectual, and emotionally poised. The character became a cultural touchstone: the refined voice of reason amid chaos, the highbrow foil to lowbrow settings, the quintessential TV sophisticate. For two decades, Grammer played Frasier with such ease that audiences rarely questioned where the character ended and the actor began. But behind the scenes, the truth was far more complex. Beneath the polished facade of a man in control was an individual quietly unraveling, grappling with emotional wounds that fame and fortune could not mend.

In many ways, the dichotomy between Kelsey Grammer's public persona and his private pain mirrored the very themes he explored in Frasier. The show often featured the title character struggling to present a composed, intellectual exterior while dealing with deep insecurities, family dysfunction, and loneliness. Grammer, too, was a man adept at putting on a performance—both on screen and off. While he accepted awards, delivered monologues, and navigated red carpets with charm and composure, he was also carrying a lifetime of trauma and sorrow few could see.

This contrast became particularly jarring during the height of Frasier's success. Audiences saw the Emmy-winning actor living the Hollywood dream: a hit series, critical acclaim, and wealth. Yet during this same period, Grammer was battling addiction, facing legal troubles, and enduring the collapse of multiple relationships. The polished image of a successful star was often maintained by sheer willpower—an act of survival as much as professionalism.

His earliest pains, rooted in childhood, were not the sort easily left behind. The murder of his father when Grammer was just thirteen was a shattering loss. Then, just seven years later, came the violent death of his younger sister, Karen, who was kidnapped, raped, and murdered in a crime that left Grammer reeling. "She was my favorite person," he later said, the pain still fresh decades on. Two half-brothers drowned in a scuba diving accident shortly afterward. Each tragedy added another layer to his grief, forming a foundation of sorrow that would inform both his personal life and his artistry.

In interviews, Grammer has spoken with quiet candor about the emotional toll of these losses. "There is a sadness that never disappears," he once said. "I know how to manage it, but I will never be rid of it." Despite his resilience, this enduring sadness bled into his personal choices—substance abuse, turbulent relationships, and periods of deep depression. While his comedic timing remained sharp on camera, his off-camera life was often clouded by heartache and volatility.

The public, conditioned to see celebrities through the lens of perfection or scandal, often missed the nuance of Grammer's situation. He was either a brilliant actor or a troubled star—rarely both. Tabloids chronicled his missteps with glee, reducing complex struggles to clickbait headlines. Few paused to consider how a man so accomplished could also be in so much pain.

This disconnect between persona and reality took a toll on Grammer's relationships as well. Friends and colleagues have noted that he could be guarded, unpredictable, and sometimes withdrawn. His marriages were fraught with conflict, and several ended in highly publicized divorces. The same man who portrayed empathy and insight on television often struggled to connect intimately in real life. It wasn't for lack of feeling—by all accounts, Grammer is a deeply emotional person—but rather a fear of vulnerability, a protective shield built out of years of hurt.

And yet, for all his missteps and emotional battles, Grammer never stopped creating. His work, in many ways, became both refuge and expression. The character of Frasier, while fictional, allowed him to explore the contradictions of being human: the desire to be understood, the difficulty of reconciling intellect and emotion, the longing for connection despite deep-seated fear. It's no coincidence that some of the show's most powerful moments are those when Frasier drops his pretense and reveals his humanity. Those moments mirrored Grammer's own struggle to be seen not just as a performer, but as a person.

Over time, the actor began to speak more openly about his struggles, slowly breaking down the wall between his public image and private reality. In doing so, he offered a rare and honest look at the cost of fame—and the courage it takes to live truthfully in its shadow. He showed that the real strength wasn't in maintaining the illusion of perfection, but in allowing others to see the pain behind the performance.

Kelsey Grammer's legacy is not just one of comedic brilliance or dramatic skill—it is also a story of resilience. In the tension between his public persona and private pain, he has become a symbol of survival, reminding us that even those who appear most put together may carry invisible wounds. And in sharing his story, Grammer offers a powerful lesson: vulnerability is not weakness—it is, perhaps, the greatest strength of all.

Friends, Foes, and Fragile Reputations

In the complicated world of Hollywood, fame often comes tethered to a high-stakes social game—one that Kelsey Grammer has played with both triumph and turbulence. His journey through the entertainment industry has not only been defined by his talents on stage and screen, but also by a revolving door of alliances and altercations, admiration and alienation. For Grammer, friendships were often hard-won and occasionally short-lived, while foes emerged from personal conflicts, public missteps, and the unforgiving court of public opinion. In the shifting landscape of stardom, his reputation proved as fragile as it was formidable.

Grammer's reputation within the entertainment community has always carried a complex duality. On one hand, colleagues have praised his genius, dedication, and command as a performer. Many actors, directors, and producers have attested to his charisma and depth, recalling moments of brilliance on set, especially during his years on Cheers and Frasier. David Hyde Pierce, who played his brother Niles, has often spoken warmly of their dynamic, describing a working relationship built on mutual respect and intuitive timing. Likewise, John Mahoney—who played their father Martin—credited Grammer's leadership as essential to the show's stability and creative excellence.

But behind the scenes, Grammer's personal struggles often complicated these professional relationships. His battles with addiction, mood swings, and erratic behavior at times placed strain on co-stars and crew members. Reports from the late 1990s described periods when Grammer would be hours late to set or emotionally volatile, especially during relapses. Though not universally condemned—many in the industry understood the deeper issues behind his behavior—his reliability was at times called into question. For an actor leading one of television's most sophisticated sitcoms, the burden of being a pillar was both professional and personal.

Grammer's troubled reputation wasn't limited to his on-set demeanor. His tumultuous personal life, especially his relationships and multiple divorces, became a public spectacle. Perhaps most notoriously, his bitter and highly publicized divorce from reality TV star Camille Grammer in the early 2010s placed his name back into tabloid rotation. The couple's acrimonious split was aired in part on The Real Housewives of Beverly Hills, where Camille painted a portrait of Grammer as emotionally distant and self-serving. While Kelsey largely refrained from engaging in a war of words in the press, the damage to his reputation was tangible. To some, he had gone from beloved sitcom star to cautionary tale—a man whose fame couldn't shield him from personal implosion.

However, the narrative surrounding Grammer was never one-sided. He also maintained long standing friendships and quietly mentored younger actors. Many who worked with him in theater or smaller film projects spoke of his generosity, his wit, and his intense commitment to the craft. Unlike many celebrities who became hardened by Hollywood, Grammer retained a certain vulnerability—a sensitivity that made him both endearing and, at times, difficult. He was a man who felt deeply, loved hard, and took slights personally, whether from friends or the media.

This sensitivity also made him fiercely loyal. Those who stood by him during his darkest hours—through rehab, arrests, and heartbreak—often found themselves rewarded with unwavering support. Grammer repay kindness with loyalty, and he never forgot those who helped him rebuild. His ability to forgive, both others and himself, became a cornerstone of his slow but steady recovery—not only from addiction, but from years of personal disintegration.

Still, even as Grammer matured and worked to repair his life, his reputation remained precarious. Public memory is notoriously fickle, especially in the realm of celebrity. For every fan who remembered him as Dr. Frasier Crane, there was another who recalled scandalous headlines, a messy divorce, or courtroom drama. The duality of admiration and criticism became a defining theme of his public life—a constant balancing act between legacy and liability.

In recent years, Grammer has taken more control over his narrative. He's spoken candidly in interviews about his regrets, his growth, and the hard-won lessons of life in the spotlight. He's also made selective returns to television and film, often with projects that reflect his more grounded, seasoned self. While not every door remained open, many in the industry embraced his return, respecting the resilience it took to endure not just the highs of fame, but its harshest laws.

"Friends, foes, it all blurs together eventually," Grammer once said in an interview. "The real challenge is being able to look in the mirror and be at peace with the man looking back." That reflection—marked by scars, wisdom, and a hard-earned sense of perspective—says more about Kelsey Grammer than any tabloid headline ever could.

His reputation, like his career, is a mosaic of contradictions: brilliance and brokenness, humor and heartache, poise and vulnerability. In the end, it's not the number of friends or foes that defines him, but his willingness to keep showing up, keep creating, and keep growing—even in the fragile, fickle world of fame.

CHAPTER 4: REINVENTION IN A RELENTLESS INDUSTRY

Producer, Director, Risk-Taker

For much of the public, Kelsey Grammer is synonymous with the character of Frasier Crane—a fast-talking psychiatrist with a penchant for opera, fine wine, and intellectual banter. But beneath the surface of that iconic role lies a man who has quietly built a multifaceted career as a producer, director, and entrepreneur. Grammer is more than an actor—he is a risk-taker who has repeatedly stepped outside the comfort zone of sitcom success to shape stories from behind the camera, champion new voices, and take creative leaps that many of his peers would shy away from. In doing so, he's carved a path marked not only by accolades, but by boldness and a restless desire to evolve.

Grammer's journey into producing began during the heyday of Frasier. As the show continued its reign over network television, Grammer grew increasingly interested in the mechanics of storytelling—not just from the actor's perspective, but from a more comprehensive, creative vantage point. He began attending writing meetings, observing production details, and engaging in high-level conversations about narrative structure and tone. His curiosity quickly turned into ambition. By the late 1990s, he had formed his own production company, Grammnet Productions, with the intention of crafting television shows that would challenge conventions and support diverse creators.

Grammnet quickly became more than a vanity label. Under Grammer's leadership, the company produced a range of television projects, including the popular and critically acclaimed series Girlfriends, a sitcom that centered around four African American women navigating careers, love, and friendship in Los Angeles. Girlfriends not only enjoyed a successful eight-season run, but also broke ground in terms of representation—an achievement that many might not have expected from the man best known for playing a Boston-based radio psychiatrist. Yet Grammer's support for the show demonstrated his willingness to defy industry expectations and use his influence to elevate stories outside of his personal experience.

This kind of risk-taking extended to his forays into directing as well. Grammer stepped behind the camera with the confidence of someone who had spent years absorbing the nuances of performance and production. Though directing episodes of Frasier was a natural first step, he also began exploring more ambitious projects in film and stage. His directorial ventures weren't always commercially successful, but they were marked by a commitment to craft and an eagerness to push creative boundaries. Whether experimenting with darker tones, edgier comedy, or political drama, Grammer showed a willingness to embrace the unknown—an uncommon trait among actors with established personas.

One of his most daring creative undertakings came with the short-lived but critically lauded Starz series Boss (2011–2012), in which Grammer not only starred as the ruthless Chicago mayor Tom Kane but also served as an executive producer. The show marked a dramatic departure from his previous roles—gone were the laughs and lightness of Frasier, replaced by corruption, deceit, and political brutality. Grammer's performance earned him a Golden Globe Award and widespread praise for his dramatic range. But more significantly, Boss demonstrated that Grammer wasn't content to rest on his sitcom laurels. He wanted to challenge himself and his audience, even if it meant venturing into unfamiliar territory.

Risk-taking, however, does not guarantee consistent rewards. Some of Grammer's projects—both in front of and behind the camera—have failed to find an audience or gain critical traction. Films such as Swing Vote or The Last Tycoon adaptation didn't ignite at the box office or in streaming numbers. Nevertheless, Grammer has remained undeterred. "You have to be willing to fall on your face," he once said. "That's the only way to learn how to fly." That willingness to stumble has kept his creative spirit alive, even when others might have chosen retirement or routine.

Beyond film and television, Grammer has also explored ventures in theater and even business, including a foray into the brewing industry with Faith American Brewing Company. These choices reflect not just a desire for profit, but a deeper need to create, to take control of his narrative, and to reinvent himself on his own terms.

In a world where many celebrities become trapped by the characters that made them famous, Grammer has consistently resisted stagnation. Whether as a producer supporting groundbreaking television, a director searching for new visual languages, or a performer redefining himself in unexpected roles, he has embodied the spirit of a true creative risk-taker. His failures have been as instructive as his successes, each one a brick in the foundation of a career built not on safety, but on evolution.

Kelsey Grammer's legacy, then, is not just one of performance, but of vision—of a man willing to leap without a net, to fail with dignity, and to rise again with renewed purpose. His willingness to take risks behind the scenes has ensured that his impact on the entertainment industry extends far beyond the sound of his voice.

Voice Work and Unexpected Roles

Kelsey Grammer is best known for his face and voice as Dr. Frasier Crane, but his talents extend far beyond that singular character. In fact, one of the most fascinating aspects of Grammer's post-Frasier career has been his dynamic range—particularly his work in voice acting and his forays into unexpected, often unconventional roles. While many actors become creatively typecast after anchoring a long-running series, Grammer used the end of Frasier not as a conclusion, but as an opportunity to diversify, surprise, and reintroduce himself to new generations of audiences.

Perhaps no voice role has become more iconic for Grammer than that of Sideshow Bob on The Simpsons. Introduced in 1990, the character is a Shakespeare-quoting, opera-loving, homicidal maniac with a vendetta against Bart Simpson—essentially, a twisted parallel of Frasier Crane. With his rich baritone and theatrical flair, Grammer brought a level of sophistication and menace to Sideshow Bob that elevated him far beyond a typical cartoon villain. His performance earned critical praise and several Emmy nominations, and the character became a fan favorite, appearing in numerous episodes over three decades.

What made Sideshow Bob such a compelling character wasn't just the absurdity of his plots, but the nuance Grammer gave him. Through a voice alone, he could project arrogance, insecurity, elegance, and insanity—all wrapped in a comedic package. It was a masterclass in vocal performance, and it solidified Grammer's place in animation history. For an actor so deeply associated with live-action television, the longevity and cultural impact of his animated alter ego proved he could thrive in virtually any medium.

Beyond The Simpsons, Grammer lent his voice to a variety of animated features and series. He voiced characters in Anastasia (1997), Toy Story 2, Storks, and Trollhunters, often playing paternal figures, villains, or eccentric oddballs. These roles allowed Grammer to explore different genres and storytelling styles—from children's fantasy to family comedy—without the physical constraints or typecasting that sometimes followed him in live-action work.

Voice acting also gave Grammer a degree of freedom that suited his complex personal life and shifting career priorities. At times when his schedule, sobriety, or family responsibilities made long on-set productions challenging, voice work offered a creative outlet that was flexible and fulfilling. And unlike the spotlight of live television, it provided a degree of anonymity and artistic experimentation he found refreshing.

But Grammer didn't stop at voice work—he also sought out unexpected and often challenging roles in film and television that broke away from his well-worn image. In 2011, he stunned both fans and critics with his dramatic turn as Mayor Tom Kane in the Starz political drama Boss. As a corrupt and terminally ill Chicago politician, Grammer was menacing, ruthless, and raw—a complete departure from the polished neuroticism of Frasier Crane. The role earned him a Golden Globe for Best Actor in a Television Series – Drama and served as a striking reminder of his dramatic capabilities.

Even more surprising were his roles in genre films and independent projects. In X-Men: The Last Stand and X-Men: Days of Future Past, Grammer portrayed Dr.

Hank McCoy, also known as Beast—a blue-furred mutant with super strength and a love of literature. It was a surprising bit of casting for a man known for urbane wit, but Grammer delivered both the physicality and the intellect required of the role, earning praise for his blend of gravitas and comic book charm.

Grammer also took chances with comedy and satire, appearing in films like The Big Empty, Down Periscope, and Like Father. While not all these projects were critical successes, they showed his willingness to embrace self-parody and venture outside the "prestige" world of highbrow sitcoms. He wasn't afraid to look silly or vulnerable, and in doing so, he broke down some of the artistic rigidity that often follows classically trained actors.

Off-screen, Grammer has spoken about his desire to constantly evolve and surprise both himself and his audience. "Acting is exploration," he once said. "It's about finding new parts of yourself through characters you never thought you'd play." That ethos has defined the latter part of his career—one built not only on reinvention but on a refusal to be boxed in by past success.

In an industry that so often confines actors to their most iconic role, Kelsey Grammer has pushed back by embracing versatility. Whether lending his legendary voice to animation, playing a mutant intellectual, or sinking his teeth into complex, morally ambiguous roles, he's demonstrated a fearlessness that separates enduring artists from fading stars.

In many ways, these voice roles and unexpected parts are emblematic of Grammer's entire journey: intelligent, unconventional, and layered with meaning. They remind us that behind the recognizable voice is a restless artist, forever searching for new ways to be heard.

Resurrecting Frasier: Nostalgia and Renewal

Few characters in television history have achieved the enduring appeal of Dr. Frasier Crane. First introduced on Cheers in 1984 and later given new life in the spin-off Frasier, the character became synonymous with sophisticated comedy, emotional complexity, and, of course, the resonant voice of Kelsey Grammer. For two decades, Frasier Crane stood as a cultural icon—an erudite oddball navigating personal turmoil through high-minded philosophy and low-stakes hilarity. So when Grammer announced plans to revive the character in a new iteration of Frasier after nearly 20 years off the air, audiences were divided between skepticism and excitement. Could lightning strike twice? Could Frasier be more than a relic of '90s television?

For Grammer, the revival was about more than ratings or nostalgia. It was deeply personal. The character of Frasier Crane had accompanied him through some of his most tumultuous years—through addiction, family tragedy, fame, and recovery. Frasier had always been more than a role; he was a creative partner, a persona that offered both distance from and insight into Grammer's own identity. Resurrecting Frasier wasn't simply about returning to familiar territory—it was about reconciling past and present, legacy and renewal.

The new series, which premiered on Paramount+ in 2023, reintroduced Frasier in a very different world. Now older, retired from radio, and navigating a new life in Boston, Frasier found himself reconnecting with his son Freddy, a blue-collar firefighter who couldn't be more different from his refined father. This generational and ideological clash became the emotional core of the reboot—allowing audiences to see a more vulnerable, human Frasier grappling with aging, family estrangement, and the changing definitions of success.

Critically, the revival walked a delicate line: it had to honor the charm and sharp wit of the original while avoiding becoming a mere echo of its former self. Grammer, now both star and executive producer, was acutely aware of this challenge. He assembled a new creative team that could bring fresh perspectives while maintaining the show's signature tone. The result was a series that paid homage to its predecessor without being enslaved by it. It dared to evolve Frasier's world—to show a man who had once defined himself by intellect and prestige now searching for purpose and connection in simpler, quieter ways.

The absence of original cast members like David Hyde Pierce (Niles) and the late John Mahoney (Martin) created emotional and structural gaps. But rather than avoid these absences, the revival acknowledged them with respect and narrative weight. The memory of Martin Crane, in particular, hung heavily over the new series, serving as a symbolic bridge between old and new. Frasier's efforts to reconnect with his son often mirrored the very tensions he once had with his own father—this time, with the roles reversed. It was a brilliant stroke of storytelling symmetry, and a testament to how thoughtfully the revival had been conceived.

Nostalgia played a key role in attracting longtime fans, but it wasn't the only ingredient. Grammer knew that in order for the show to have longevity, it had to resonate with new viewers as well. To that end, the reboot introduced new characters, settings, and conflicts that reflected today's cultural climate—while still wrapping them in the show's classic blend of irony, intellect, and emotional insight. The result was not merely a revival, but a reinvention: a show about legacy that was actively creating a new one.

In interviews surrounding the launch, Grammer often described the new Frasier as "a story about second acts." That sentiment applied as much to the character as to himself. For a man who had weathered public and private storms, revisiting Frasier offered a chance to reflect on how far he'd come—and how far he still wanted to go. It was not about repeating past glories, but proving that growth, humor, and relevance were still within reach.

Commercially, the revival found moderate success—not the ratings juggernaut of the original, but a solid performer with loyal viewership. More importantly, it sparked conversations about the value of character-driven television in a media landscape increasingly dominated by spectacle. Frasier had always been about conversation—witty, neurotic, sometimes pretentious, but always sincere. And in reviving it, Grammer reminded audiences of the power of dialogue, both scripted and unscripted.

Ultimately, Resurrecting Frasier was about more than nostalgia. It was an exploration of identity in later life, a meditation on the father-son dynamic, and a showcase for one of television's most enduring performers reclaiming the role that made him a household name. In bringing Frasier Crane back to life, Kelsey Grammer also offered himself—and his audience—a chance to believe in the enduring power of reinvention.

CHAPTER 5: FAITH, FAMILY, AND FORWARD MOTION

Spiritual Anchors and Personal Redemption

Kelsey Grammer's life has been a study in extremes—soaring professional success matched by heartbreaking personal tragedy, public adoration contrasted with tabloid scandal. Yet through the shifting tides of fame and adversity, one constant has emerged in Grammer's journey: a deeply held, often quietly expressed spiritual faith. For Grammer, religion has not been a performance or a public platform, but rather a private compass, a place of grounding when everything else—career, family, identity—has seemed to fracture. His story of personal redemption is inseparable from his spiritual beliefs, which have played a critical role in shaping not only the man he has become, but the choices he continues to make.

Grammer's early life gave him little sense of stability or security. The murders of his father and sister, the drowning deaths of his twin half-brothers, and a series of personal losses created a landscape of emotional chaos.

In interviews, Grammer has admitted that in the face of such suffering, he turned to numbing behaviors—drugs, alcohol, and impulsive relationships—as a means of escaping grief that felt insurmountable. But amid the turmoil, there were also moments of introspection and spiritual searching. Grammer was raised in a loosely Christian household, but it wasn't until adulthood that faith became something he claimed for himself—not as dogma, but as dialogue with something greater.

One of the most pivotal periods in his spiritual awakening came during his repeated struggles with addiction. Grammer entered rehab multiple times over the years, but it wasn't until the late 2000s that he began to openly discuss how faith and sobriety were deeply intertwined for him. He often credited a "renewed relationship with God" as the bedrock of his recovery, describing prayer as a daily act of both surrender and strength. His concept of faith wasn't limited to church attendance or religious rituals; instead, it became a personal framework for accountability, humility, and healing.

This transformation wasn't instantaneous or without relapse. Like many who grapple with addiction, Grammer's road to redemption was messy and nonlinear. Yet he emerged from his lowest points with a changed perspective—one that valued family, integrity, and emotional honesty over fame or escapism. In his public appearances and interviews, there was a noticeable shift: less bravado, more vulnerability. He began speaking not only of past mistakes, but of the gratitude he felt for having survived them. "I don't think God saved me because I'm special," he once said. "I think He saved me because I finally started listening."

One of the most visible ways Grammer has embodied his faith is through his work. He has produced and acted in several films and stage productions with spiritual or redemptive themes, including the 2019 film Jesus Revolution, where he portrayed a real-life pastor during the countercultural Christian revival of the 1970s. His performance was heartfelt and subdued, free from theatrics or preachiness. It felt like a personal offering, a merging of his craft and convictions. For Grammer, acting has often been a sacred act—a form of expression that allows him to explore the moral and emotional struggles that define the human condition.

But perhaps the most profound evidence of his personal redemption lies in the quieter aspects of his life: his enduring marriage to Kayte Walsh, his devotion to his children, and his willingness to mend broken relationships. After years of high-profile divorces and public feuds, Grammer has embraced a more grounded, intentional way of living. He speaks often of the peace he's found in family dinners, quiet mornings, and moments of spiritual reflection. In this slower rhythm, he's found a kind of freedom that eluded him during his meteoric rise.

He has also used his voice—literally and figuratively—to advocate for causes that align with his personal beliefs. From supporting programs for addiction recovery to speaking about trauma and healing, Grammer has sought to use his platform with more responsibility in recent years. His message is rarely self-righteous or moralizing. Rather, it's rooted in experience: that pain can be a teacher, that brokenness doesn't have to be permanent, and that redemption is always possible—however long it takes.

Grammer's story is not about perfection. It's about perseverance. It's about a man who has known the highest highs and lowest lows, and who has come to see faith not as a shield against suffering, but as a way through it. His spiritual anchors have allowed him to rebuild his life brick by brick, and to embrace the work of becoming whole—not for an audience, but for himself.

In the grand narrative of celebrity culture, redemption stories can sometimes feel forced or scripted. But Kelsey Grammer's path feels authentic because it is ongoing. His spiritual journey is not finished. It is still being written—one choice, one prayer, one performance at a time.

Love, Loss, and Life After the Storm

For Kelsey Grammer, the journey through fame, trauma, addiction, and redemption has always been shadowed and, at times, illuminated—by love. Love in his life has come in many forms: romantic relationships, deep friendships, familial bonds, and spiritual grace. But it has also been tested by extraordinary loss. To understand Grammer's life after the storm is to understand how love has both hurt him and healed him—how, in spite of the wreckage, he has built something enduring out of the pieces.

Grammer's early encounters with love were marked by longing and absence. The murders of his father and younger sister—brutal, senseless acts—left behind not only grief, but a hole in his understanding of what safe, permanent love looked like. These wounds, unprocessed and deeply buried, would haunt his future relationships. As a young man, he clung to romantic partnerships with a desperation born of loss. But as is often the case when love becomes a stand-in for healing, many of these relationships were fraught, passionate, and ultimately unsustainable.

The public watched as Grammer's personal life unfolded in headlines: multiple marriages, affairs, high-profile divorces. His most infamous relationship was with Camille Donatacci, a former dancer and reality TV star.

Their marriage, already rocky, became tabloid fodder during the filming of The Real Housewives of Beverly Hills. By the time their bitter divorce played out on national television in 2010, Grammer was once again cast in the role of the troubled star unable to maintain personal happiness.

But beneath the surface of scandal was a man still trying to find peace and stability. Grammer has often said that his pattern of failed relationships stemmed not from selfishness, but from confusion—an inability to reconcile the love he craved with the love he believed he deserved. "I used to think love had to be dramatic to be real," he once confessed. "But drama is just noise. Real love is quiet. It's patient."

This realization came, in part, through his relationship with Kayte Walsh, a British flight attendant 25 years his junior. Their courtship was initially met with skepticism and media scrutiny, but over time, it proved to be the healthiest and most enduring relationship of Grammer's adult life. The couple married in 2011 and have since had three children together. In interviews, Grammer frequently credits Kayte with bringing calm to his once-chaotic world. "She saved me," he's said—not in a romanticized, storybook way, but through consistent presence and quiet support.

Their marriage marked a turning point for Grammer not just romantically, but emotionally and spiritually. For the first time, he appeared to be living a life built on balance, not bravado. The love he had once chased now seemed to be something he cultivated. He became more involved in his children's lives, choosing roles that allowed for stability and family time. Home, once elusive, became real.

But even in this season of calm, loss remained a constant shadow. The deaths that defined his youth would never fully loosen their grip. He has spoken movingly about how grief reappears in moments both expected and sudden—a piece of music, a smell, the way a child laughs. And yet, he doesn't view grief as the enemy. "Grief is love that doesn't know where to go," he said. "It lives with you. But it doesn't have to define you."

In his later years, Grammer has embraced the idea that healing is not linear. Life after the storm doesn't mean life without pain—it means life with perspective. The man who once drowned sorrow in drugs and drink now faces it with mindfulness and, when needed, faith. He is a father of seven, a grandfather, a husband, and a man who has finally learned how to be alone without being lonely.

Professionally, this new era of his life has seen him take on more selective projects—roles that reflect maturity, introspection, and nuance. He has also become an advocate for causes close to his heart, including child welfare, mental health awareness, and addiction recovery. In sharing his story publicly, Grammer has given others permission to speak their own truths, to move forward despite—or because of—the pain they've endured.

In the end, Kelsey Grammer's story is not just about fame or tragedy. It is about survival—and the strange, beautiful rebirth that can follow devastation. Love, in all its forms, has wounded him and saved him. Loss has broken him and taught him how to rebuild. And life, in its messy unpredictability, has given him the kind of wisdom that only storms can carve into a man.

Grammer's journey reminds us that no matter how dark the past, love and light are always possible—not in the absence of pain, but because of it.

The Enduring Power of Purpose

As Kelsey Grammer moves through the later stages of his life and career, one theme resonates above all others: purpose. More than fame, more than fortune, more than redemption alone, it is the purpose that has sustained him—steadily, silently—through triumph and tragedy alike. For Grammer, purpose is not a singular achievement or destination. It is a practice, an evolving guidepost that gives meaning to pain, context to success, and motivation to keep going even when the world is watching—and especially when it isn't.

In his early years, purpose was wrapped up in survival. Orphaned by violence and separated by grief, a young Grammer found refuge in storytelling, finding in the stage a sanctuary from the chaos of real life. Shakespeare gave him structure; acting gave him identity. In drama, he discovered the power of embodying another life—a paradoxical way to find his own. The stage wasn't just an outlet for creativity; it was a lifeline. Acting gave him purpose when little else made sense, and it became the framework around which his young adulthood was built.

As his star rose, purpose seemed to evolve into ambition. In his Frasier Crane years—spanning two decades and two series—Grammer became a household name, won multiple Emmy Awards, and ascended to the highest ranks of American television. But with success came pressure. He has since acknowledged that, during those years, he often mistook momentum for meaning. "I thought if I just kept working, I'd outrun everything else," he once admitted. "But purpose isn't just about being busy. It's about being present."

When addiction, legal troubles, and personal losses brought his life to a halt, Grammer was forced to reassess not just what he was doing—but why. These were not just moments of crisis; they were crossroads. And what emerged from them wasn't simply recovery—it was reinvention. He came to understand that purpose couldn't be borrowed from applause or defined by roles. It had to be self-sustained. That revelation marked the beginning of a more grounded, conscious chapter in his life.

This sense of renewed purpose has manifested in a number of ways: in his commitment to his family, in his advocacy work, in the projects he now chooses to produce and perform in. In recent years, Grammer has become more selective, gravitating toward stories that reflect personal transformation, spiritual questions, and emotional authenticity. Whether voicing animated characters, returning to the stage, or resurrecting Frasier for a new generation, he is guided less by popularity and more by passion. His work, though still in the public eye, now feels deeply personal.

One of the clearest signs of his matured sense of purpose is his devotion to fatherhood. After years of strained or complicated relationships with his older children, Grammer has fully embraced the role of being a present, engaged parent to his youngest kids. He speaks with tenderness and pride about school pickups, bedtime stories, and the quiet joys of family life—rituals that once felt out of reach during the chaos of his earlier fame. Purpose, now, includes these simple but profound moments of connection.

But the purpose for Grammer also extends beyond the personal. He has used his voice and resources to support charitable causes, particularly those related to addiction recovery, veterans' mental health, and trauma healing. Having walked those difficult paths himself, Grammer understands the power of visibility and vulnerability. By sharing his story, he offers a kind of companionship to those still in the struggle, proving that survival is not only possible, but also meaningful. In doing so, he transforms personal pain into collective hope.

Spiritually, purpose has become a guiding force in Grammer's life. His faith, though private, is deeply rooted, offering him a framework for understanding not just the suffering he has endured, but the responsibility he carries as a public figure. "I've been given a lot," he once said. "Not because I'm better—but maybe because I'm supposed to do something with it." This sense of stewardship—of turning his life experience into something useful for others—has become an essential component of his later-life philosophy.

Purpose has also shaped his outlook on aging. Unlike many in Hollywood, Grammer does not shy away from the realities of getting older. Instead, he sees it as a privilege denied to many he has lost. With age has come perspective, humility, and, perhaps most importantly, the ability to appreciate his journey not in spite of its messiness, but because of it. "I used to think the purpose was what I did," he noted in a recent interview. "Now I think it's more about who I am becoming."

In the end, Kelsey Grammer's legacy will not rest solely on his awards or performances, but on the larger narrative of transformation and resilience he has lived out in the public eye. His story is not a neat arc, but a living document—full of setbacks and comebacks, brokenness and beauty. Through it all, purpose has been the throughline, the engine, the quiet force that moved him forward when nothing else could.

And perhaps that is the most enduring truth of all: that in finding and holding onto purpose, Kelsey Grammer has not only saved his life—he has given it meaning.

CONCLUSION: THE ECHO OF A SINGULAR LIFE

Legacy Etched in Laughter and Pain

Few public figures wear their contradictions as openly as Kelsey Grammer. He is, at once, the brilliant comic actor whose voice became synonymous with wit and refinement—and the haunted soul who survived more personal loss than most can imagine. His name conjures laughter for many, particularly for the millions who invited Dr. Frasier Crane into their homes over two decades. But beneath the elegance of that fictional persona lies a man whose real life has been marked by chaos, grief, resilience, and, ultimately, reinvention. Grammer's legacy, then, is not a singular note struck on a flawless instrument. It is a complex melody composed in laughter and pain—each informing the other.

The laughter came first, or at least it became the most recognizable part of his public identity. Cheers and Frasier defined a television era, with Grammer's portrayal of the erudite, neurotic psychiatrist becoming one of the most iconic and enduring characters in sitcom history. With impeccable timing and a voice that could blend arrogance with absurdity, he brought Frasier Crane to life in a way that transcended the screen. Audiences laughed with him, at him, and sometimes despite him. That laughter—sophisticated, layered, human—helped shape a generation of television comedy.

But even as he earned accolades and cemented his place in pop culture, the pain was never far behind. Grammer's personal history reads like a litany of heartbreak: his father shot to death when Kelsey was just 13; his sister abducted, raped, and murdered a few years later; his twin half-brothers lost in a diving accident. These tragedies were not mere background noise—they were formative. They haunted his relationships, fueled his addictions, and cast long shadows over his brightest days. And yet, they also deepened his art. Every comedic beat he mastered, every dramatic line he delivered, was filtered through a man who had known what it meant to suffer.

In the tradition of the great tragicomic performers Charlie Chaplin, Robin Williams, Richard Pryor Grammer learned to transmute personal pain into artistic truth. He never let grief become a gimmick, but neither did he shy away from its impact. His performances, even in the zaniest sitcom moments, carried a certain emotional weight. When Frasier Crane stumbled through heartbreak or wrestled with his own ego, there was something more behind the punchlines—a real human being grappling with the same disappointments, insecurities, and longings as the audience. That authenticity is part of what made his comedy feel not only sharp but sincere.

As the years wore on, Grammer's battles became increasingly public. His substance abuse, his legal troubles, his turbulent love life—each was dissected in tabloids and interviews. Yet even in these lowest points, he never abandoned his craft. In fact, some of his most powerful performances, particularly on stage and in voice work, came during periods of personal turmoil. The voice that had made people laugh now began to tell different kinds of stories—of survival, of struggle, of faith. He wasn't just making people laugh anymore; he was helping them feel.

What makes Grammer's legacy so compelling is not the contradiction between his triumphs and tragedies, but the way he has learned to hold both in the same hand. He doesn't run from his past, nor does he dwell in it. He tells the truth—sometimes with humor, sometimes with raw honesty—about what it means to live a life both blessed and burdened. He has spoken candidly about how loss nearly destroyed him, how love has rebuilt him, and how purpose continues to guide him. In this way, his legacy is not just a résumé of roles and awards, but a living testimony to endurance.

His influence extends beyond the screen. As a producer, director, and voice actor, Grammer has helped shape stories that reflect the complexities of the human experience. As a husband and father, he has recommitted himself to creating the kind of stability he was so often denied in his own youth. As a public figure, he has allowed his vulnerabilities to serve a larger message: that healing is possible, that humor can be a balm, and that no life is too fractured to be made whole.

In the end, Kelsey Grammer's life cannot be summed up by a single role, a singular tragedy, or even a singular redemption. His is a legacy built over decades, carved through pain and polished through perseverance. He is a man who has made people laugh until they cried—and whose own tears have never been far from the surface.

That is the enduring power of his story: that it doesn't shy away from the darkness, but invites us to find the light anyway. His legacy is not perfect—but it is honest, courageous, and deeply human. And for that, it is unforgettable.

A Voice That Transcended Generations

Kelsey Grammer's voice is instantly recognizable, rich, resonant, and steeped in the kind of authority that can only come from experience. For decades, that voice has been a comforting constant for audiences spanning multiple generations. Whether it was offering pompous advice as Frasier Crane, delivering dry wit in animated roles, or reciting Shakespeare on stage, Grammer's vocal signature became more than a tool of performance. It became a cultural artifact—a voice that transcended the characters, the scripts, and even time itself.

The power of Grammer's voice lies not merely in its tone but in its versatility. He has used it to portray a wide range of personas: the aloof psychiatrist, the animated supervillain, the tragic stage king, the warm narrator. In each case, the voice adapted while retaining its unmistakable core. It could be comedic or commanding, theatrical or intimate. In a world increasingly dominated by fast-cut visuals and fleeting attention, Grammer's voice had the unique power to slow time, to draw people in, to make words matter.

Frasier Crane, the role that defined Grammer's career, was arguably inseparable from the voice that brought him to life. That baritone—clipped, articulate, slightly pretentious—became a character in itself. It wasn't just what Frasier said, but how he said it: the flair of enunciation, the musicality of phrasing, the barely concealed exasperation or inflated pride. Through Frasier, Grammer gave voice to a kind of humor that was both intellectual and absurd. His delivery turned overwritten dialogue into accessible entertainment. He made people laugh not just at jokes, but at rhythm, cadence, and tone.

But Grammer's vocal influence extended far beyond the sitcom set. He was, and remains, one of the most sought-after voice actors in Hollywood. His turn as Sideshow Bob on The Simpsons is a masterclass in character voicing—menacing, grandiloquent, and hilarious all at once. Through that role, Grammar showcased his ability to make even villainy charming, threading Shakespearean gravitas through an animated lens. His readings of literature and poetry, his narration of documentaries, and his frequent guest appearances in animated series cemented his reputation not just as an actor, but as a voice that could carry emotion, story, and sophistication in equal measure.

Generations grew up with that voice in their homes. Baby boomers met him on Cheers; Gen Xers embraced Frasier; Millennials laughed at Sideshow Bob; Gen Z discovered him anew in reboots and streaming platforms. Few performers have had that kind of cross-generational appeal, and even fewer have sustained it primarily through vocal work. Grammer's voice transcended generational barriers not by changing itself, but by remaining true to its essence: expressive, intelligent, and grounded in emotional truth.

That enduring voice also became a metaphor for Grammer himself—a symbol of his survival. In interviews, podcasts, and even in courtrooms, his voice remained steady even when his life did not. After personal losses, addiction, and public controversy, he continued to speak with thoughtfulness, clarity, and self-awareness. That vocal steadiness became part of his personal narrative: here was a man who had been through it all and still had something to say—still had the voice to say it with.

There is also something deeply human about Grammer's voice. It is not artificially smoothed or aggressively modernized. It carries the timbre of age, of experience, of stories lived and learned. Unlike many performers who attempt to remain forever youthful in their sound and speech, Grammer has allowed his voice to age naturally, and in doing so, he has become an even more trusted narrator of human experience. As a result, audiences feel a kind of intimacy with him, as if they are listening to someone who has seen the world's highs and lows and has chosen, still, to speak kindly and wisely about it.

The legacy of that voice goes beyond entertainment. It is preserved in reruns, audiobooks, and archived recordings. But more importantly, it lives in memory. For many, Grammer's voice is linked to formative years, late-night comfort, family laughter, and solitary reflection. It is the voice of father figures, flawed heroes, tragic clowns, and, most poignantly, survivors.

In an age where so much noise competes for attention, a voice like Kelsey Grammer's stands apart—not because it shouts, but because it resonates. It reminds us of the power of language, of delivery, of presence. It carries not just words, but meaning. Not just characters, but lives.

In the end, the voice that once made us laugh now also helps us remember. And that, perhaps, is its greatest legacy: not just that we heard it—but that we still listen.

Beyond the Screen: The Triumph of Becoming Whole

For most of his career, Kelsey Grammer was known for what he portrayed: the affable intellectual, the flawed comedic hero, the animated antagonist, the booming narrator. He was a performer in every sense—beloved for his ability to slip into roles that entertained and enchanted. But the real triumph of his life didn't happen on television sets or theater stages. It happened off-camera, far from scripted lines and standing ovations. It happened slowly, painfully, and ultimately triumphantly, as he wrestled with the fractured pieces of his past and began the lifelong work of becoming whole.

Grammer's life is often described as a contradiction: a man who made millions laugh while enduring immeasurable sorrow; a television icon plagued by private demons; a voice of reason on-screen who lived through chaos off of it. And yet, perhaps these contradictions are not opposites, but mirrors—reflecting a journey that was never about pretending to be perfect, but about learning to live with imperfection. That is the triumph: not in being untouched by pain, but in integrating it into a fuller sense of self.

Off-screen, Grammer's journey toward wholeness was messy and nonlinear. The deaths of his father and sister in acts of violence could have frozen him in grief. His years of addiction and troubled relationships could have buried his career, his reputation, or even his life. But instead of remaining stuck in those darkest places, Grammer choose—again and again—to confront them. Sometimes that meant therapy. Sometimes it meant faith. Sometimes it meant simply staying alive for another day. It was never one grand transformation, but a thousand small decisions: to forgive, to speak, to grow, to stay.

What makes Grammer's evolution particularly compelling is his increasing willingness to tell the truth about it. In interviews, he has spoken candidly about his struggles—not with self-pity, but with perspective. He doesn't deny the hurt, the harm, or the havoc he at times brought into his own life. But he doesn't let them define him either. By owning his flaws, he has reclaimed his story. That vulnerability is a different kind of strength—one that reaches beyond the screen to connect with anyone who has ever felt broken, lost, or ashamed.

Faith became a cornerstone in this path to becoming whole. While Grammer has never made a spectacle of his beliefs, he has credited his spirituality as a major force in helping him rebuild. "There has to be something bigger than the pain," he once said. For him, that "something" is God—a quiet presence that offered him hope, discipline, and the sense that his suffering had not been in vain. Faith didn't erase his trauma, but it reframed it. Through grace, he found the courage to stop running from the past and start living in the present.

Family, too, has been essential to this transformation. After decades marked by romantic instability and estrangement, Grammer has emerged as a devoted husband and father. His later-in-life marriage to Kayte Walsh and the birth of their children offered him the grounding he long sought but rarely found. These aren't the scenes captured in tabloids or headlines—but they are the ones that matter most. Quiet mornings, bedtime stories, shared meals—these became the new markers of success, the rituals of a man who finally understood that presence was more powerful than performance.

Professionally, Grammer's pursuit of wholeness led him to new kinds of roles and creative risks. He took on characters with more depth, produced stories that dealt with redemption, and lent his voice to projects that resonated with deeper truths. Even the decision to revisit Frasier was not one of nostalgia alone—it was a chance to reflect on change, aging, and second acts. Through his work, he offered not just entertainment, but echoes of his own journey—reminders that people can evolve, that identities can be reshaped, that healing is possible.

And perhaps that's what becoming whole really means—not arriving at a perfect endpoint, but embracing every part of the journey. Grammer will never be untouched by the traumas of his youth, the mistakes of his past, or the costs of his fame. But he is no longer defined by them. He is a man who has fallen and stood again, not once, but many times. A man who found his voice, lost it, and found it again—this time not just to perform, but to speak his truth.

Beyond the screen, beyond the roles, beyond the legend of Frasier Crane, Kelsey Grammer's true triumph is in becoming himself—fully, painfully, beautifully. Whole not because he is without cracks, but because he has made peace with them. And in doing so, he offers us all a powerful reminder: that wholeness isn't about erasing the scars. It's about wearing them with grace.

Printed in Dunstable, United Kingdom

66519405R00060